for the 2010 Michaelhouse Festival
under the auspices of the University Church of St Mary the Grea

The Gift of Charity

JOHN RUTTER

Words by Selwyn Image
based on I Corinthians 13

Printed in Great Britain

OXFORD UNIVERSITY PRESS MUSIC DEPARTMENT, GREAT CLARENDON STREET, OXFORD OX2 6DP

4

SACRED
SATB and organ

JOHN RUTTER
THE GIFT OF CHARITY

John Rutter CBE was born in London in 1945 and studied music at Clare College, Cambridge. His compositions embrace choral, orchestral, and instrumental music, and he has edited or co-edited various choral anthologies, including four *Carols for Choirs* volumes with Sir David Willcocks and the *Oxford Choral Classics* series. He now divides his time between composition and conducting and is sought after as a guest conductor for the world's leading choirs and orchestras.

HAVE YOU TRIED?

I am with you always (ISBN 978-0-19-336879-8)
Look to the day (ISBN 978-0-19-336012-9)
Most glorious Lord of life (ISBN 978-0-19-337646-5)
To every thing there is a season (ISBN 978-0-19-336275-8)

For more details about John Rutter and his music, please contact Oxford University Press, Music Department.

OXFORD
UNIVERSITY PRESS

www.oup.com

ISBN 978-0-19-337645-8

9 780193 376458